Primal Pursuits

Unraveling the Secrets of Human Survival and Mating

Freudian Trips

Copyright Page

Disclaimer

The views and opinions expressed in this book are those of the author(s) and do not necessarily reflect the official policy or position of any other agency, organization, employer, or company. The contents of this book are for informational and educational purposes only and are not intended to serve as professional advice, diagnosis, or treatment.

The information provided in this book is believed to be accurate and reliable as of the date of publication. However, it may include some errors or inaccuracies, and no warranty or guarantee is provided regarding the accuracy, timeliness, or applicability of the content.

Readers are encouraged to consult with professional philosophers, educators, or other qualified professionals where appropriate for personalized advice. The author(s) and publisher shall not be liable for any loss, damage, or harm caused or alleged to be caused, directly or indirectly, by the information or ideas contained, suggested, or referenced in this book.

By reading this book, the reader acknowledges and agrees that they are solely responsible for how they interpret and apply the information contained herein.

This book may also include references to other works, studies, and sources. These references are provided for further reading and exploration and do not imply endorsement or validation of the specific theories, viewpoints, or interpretations presented in those works.

Chapter I: The Roadmap to Understanding Human Behavior

In this chapter, we'll embark on a fascinating journey into the world of evolutionary psychology. Don't worry if you're not a psychology expert; we'll keep things simple and engaging so that everyone can grasp the concepts.

A. Defining Evolutionary Psychology

Imagine this: you're in a room filled with people from all over the world. Some speak different languages, have different backgrounds, and follow different traditions. It's a diverse crowd, yet they all share something in common: they're human beings.

Evolutionary psychology is like the Rosetta Stone for understanding human behavior. It's the key that helps us decipher why we do the things we do, even though we come from different backgrounds. So, what exactly is it?

Evolutionary psychology is a way of thinking about why we act the way we do by looking at our past. It's like being a detective, but instead of solving crimes, we're figuring out why we love, hate, fear, and cooperate. You see, just like birds build nests and spiders spin webs, humans have behaviors that have been shaped over a looooong time – millions of years! These behaviors helped our ancestors survive and reproduce, and they're still with us today.

B. The Significance of Survival and Mating

Now, let's talk about two big themes: survival and mating. These two things are like the yin and yang of evolutionary psychology.

Survival is all about staying alive. Imagine our ancient ancestors facing dangers like saber-toothed tigers or harsh weather. They had to make quick decisions to survive – fight or flee, eat or starve. Our brains are wired to make those decisions too, even in our modern, less dangerous world. Think about how you might jump when you hear a loud noise – that's your survival instinct at work!

Mating, on the other hand, is about finding a partner and having babies. Again, our ancestors were the pros at this, and their strategies for finding the right mate were critical. They had to pick someone who would help them have strong, healthy offspring. Even today, we find certain traits attractive because they're connected to being good partners and parents.

C. The Evolutionary Perspective on Human Behavior

Now, let's put it all together. Imagine you have a big puzzle, and each piece represents a little part of human behavior. Evolutionary psychology is like the picture on the puzzle box – it helps us see how all the pieces fit together.

So, when you see someone being kind to others, it's not just random. It's because being nice helped our ancestors build strong social groups that offered protection and resources. When you see someone being cautious in a dark alley, it's not just paranoia. It's our survival instinct telling us to be careful.

In this book, we'll explore these behaviors and more, discovering the ancient roots behind our everyday actions. We'll uncover how our brains have evolved to solve problems, adapt to challenges, and navigate the tricky world of survival and mating.

So, fasten your seatbelts, because we're about to embark on a thrilling journey through the fascinating world of evolutionary psychology, where the past and present come together to reveal the secrets of why we humans do what we do.

Chapter II: The Building Blocks of Evolutionary Psychology

Welcome back to our exploration of evolutionary psychology! In this chapter, we're going to lay down the fundamental ideas that make this field so exciting and eye-opening. We promise to keep things simple and engaging, so everyone can join the adventure.

A. Darwin's Legacy: Natural Selection

First up, let's talk about a guy named Charles Darwin. You might have heard of him; he's the one who came up with the theory of evolution. But what's evolution got to do with psychology? Well, a lot!

Imagine a world where animals and plants are like characters in a never-ending story. Some creatures are born with traits that help them survive and have babies, while others aren't so lucky. Over time, the lucky ones with the helpful traits have more babies, and their traits get passed down to the next generation. This process is called natural selection.

Think of it as a game of "Survival of the Fittest." The creatures with the best traits for their environment get to stick around and have more babies. Eventually, these traits become common in the population because they give a better chance at survival.

Now, apply this idea to humans. Our ancestors faced all sorts of challenges, like finding food, escaping predators, and staying healthy. Natural selection favored those who had traits that helped them tackle these challenges. So, in a way, our brains and behaviors have been shaped by millions of years of this "survival game."

B. The Role of Genes in Human Behavior

Genes, those tiny things inside our cells, play a crucial role in this story. They're like the instruction manuals that tell our bodies and brains how to work. And guess what? These instruction manuals can influence our behavior too!

Think of it like a recipe book. Each recipe (gene) tells you how to make a different dish (trait or behavior). For example, there's a "recipe" for eye color, and there are "recipes" that can influence how friendly or anxious you are. These genes can be inherited from your parents, and they contribute to what makes you, well, you.

But here's the twist: genes don't control everything. They're more like guidelines. They create a range of possibilities for our traits and behaviors, but other factors, like our environment and experiences, can also shape who we become. So, it's not just nature (genes) but also nurture (our experiences) that makes us who we are.

C. The Adaptationist Approach

Now, let's talk about the adaptationist approach. This is a fancy term that basically means looking at things from an evolutionary perspective. It's like trying to solve a puzzle by thinking about how each piece fits into the bigger picture.

Picture this: Imagine you have a toolbox filled with different tools. Each tool has a specific job, like a screwdriver for turning screws or a wrench for tightening bolts. In the same way, our traits and behaviors are like tools that help us survive and thrive in our environment.

The adaptationist approach asks questions like, "Why do we get angry?" or "Why do we fall in love?" It tries to find out how these behaviors helped our ancestors survive and pass on their genes. So, when we see someone getting angry, we can think of it as a tool that helped our ancestors defend themselves or protect their loved ones.

In this book, we'll use these three fundamental ideas—natural selection, genes, and the adaptationist approach—to unravel the mysteries of human behavior. We'll explore how evolution has left its mark on our minds and bodies, shaping who we are today. So, get ready to dig deeper into the fascinating world of evolutionary psychology and discover the incredible ways in which our past influences our present.

Chapter III: Survival Instincts: From Caveman to Modern Human

Welcome to the heart-pounding world of survival instincts! In this chapter, we'll journey through time, from the days of cavemen to the hustle and bustle of modern life, exploring how our ancient survival strategies still influence us today. We'll keep things simple and exciting, so everyone can dive into the adventure.

A. The Evolution of Fear and Anxiety

Survival Strategies in Prehistoric Times

Close your eyes and imagine you're a caveman or cavewoman. You live in a world filled with wild beasts, unpredictable weather, and mysterious dangers lurking in the shadows. In this challenging environment, your ancestors needed some serious survival skills.

One of the greatest tools they had was fear and anxiety. When a rustle in the bushes sent their hearts racing, it was a sign that danger might be nearby. Fear would trigger a "fight or flight" response, helping them decide whether to stand their ground and fight or make a run for it. This quick decision-making saved lives.

Fast forward to today, and we still have this ancient survival instinct. When you feel that unease before an important presentation or when you hesitate to enter a dark alley, it's your body's way of preparing you to deal with potential threats. So, fear and anxiety are like the body's emergency alarm system, honed over millions of years.

Modern Manifestations of Survival Instincts

Now, think about your everyday life. You may not be running from saber-toothed tigers, but modern life is still filled with challenges. Your brain has adapted to these new situations using the same old instincts.

For example, the fear of social rejection may have roots in the need to belong to a group for safety. The fear of failing at work might stem from the need to provide for your family. And the anxiety about health issues could be a modern twist on the ancient fear of illness.

So, while the dangers have changed, our ancient survival instincts are still at work, keeping us alert and ready to face whatever life throws our way.

B. The Quest for Food and Resources

Scarcity, Hoarding, and Consumer Behavior

Now, let's shift our focus to another primal instinct: the quest for food and resources. Back in the day, our ancestors had to be vigilant about finding enough food to survive. They learned to spot opportunities and grab resources whenever they could.

This instinct to secure resources sometimes led to behaviors like hoarding. Imagine you're a prehistoric hunter-gatherer, and you find a berry patch. You wouldn't just eat a few berries and move on; you'd stock up because you didn't know when the next meal would come along.

In the modern world, this instinct still influences us. Ever catch yourself stockpiling snacks, clothes, or gadgets, even when you don't really need them? That's your ancient hoarding instinct showing itself. It's like your brain's way of saying, "Better safe than sorry."

The Role of Technology in Resource Acquisition

Nowadays, we don't hunt mammoths or gather berries, but we do hunt for other kinds of resources, like money and information. Our brains have adapted to the digital age, and technology has become our hunting ground.

Think about online shopping, for instance. It's like going on a treasure hunt, searching for the best deals and rare finds. And when you discover a great deal or a hard-to-find item, you get a little rush of satisfaction – just like our ancestors felt when they found food.

In this fast-paced world, technology has given us new ways to gather resources and meet our needs. But underneath it all, our ancient instincts for resource acquisition are still guiding our behavior.

In this chapter, we've explored how our primal survival instincts, honed through millions of years of evolution, continue to shape our thoughts and actions in the modern world. Whether it's the anxiety that keeps us alert or the drive to secure resources, these ancient instincts are the hidden forces behind many of our daily choices. So, as we journey through this book, keep an eye out for these survival instincts in action, and you'll see just how deep our primal roots go.

Chapter IV: The Intricate World of Mating

Get ready for a captivating journey into the complex world of mating, where love, attraction, and relationships have deep roots in our evolutionary history. We'll keep things simple and engaging, so everyone can follow along on this exciting exploration.

A. The Evolution of Sexual Reproduction

Sexual Selection and Mate Preferences

Let's start at the beginning: the story of sexual reproduction. Unlike some creatures that can reproduce all on their own, humans need a partner to create offspring. This partnership is a dance that has evolved over time.

Imagine a dance competition where everyone is trying to impress a partner. In the world of nature, this is called sexual selection. Animals and humans alike have developed traits and behaviors that make them more attractive to potential mates.

So, why do you find certain traits attractive? It turns out that what we're drawn to often has a lot to do with what might make a good partner. For example, if you're looking for a long-term relationship, you might be attracted to someone who seems reliable and kind. But if you're more interested in a short-term fling, you might be drawn to someone with physical attractiveness.

The Biological Basis of Attraction

Attraction isn't just about what's on the surface; it's deeply rooted in our biology. When you feel that fluttery feeling in your stomach around someone you like, it's not just random. Your brain is releasing chemicals like dopamine and oxytocin, which make you feel good and build a connection with that person.

These biological reactions have been fine-tuned over generations to help us choose suitable partners for reproduction and long-term bonding. So, when you're attracted to someone, it's your body's way of saying, "Hey, this person might be a good match for creating strong, healthy offspring."

B. Strategies for Reproductive Success

Short-Term vs. Long-Term Mating Strategies

Now, let's talk about mating strategies. Just like in a game of chess, people have different strategies when it comes to finding a mate. Some folks prefer the short-term mating strategy, where they're looking for a fun and casual connection. Others go for the long-term mating strategy, seeking a committed and stable relationship.

These strategies have their roots in our evolutionary history. For some, spreading their genes far and wide was the best approach, while others focused on nurturing and protecting their offspring. It's like two different paths to reproductive success, and both have their advantages and trade-offs.

Male and Female Reproductive Strategies

Men and women often have slightly different strategies when it comes to mating. This doesn't mean one is better than the other; it's just a reflection of how our ancestors approached reproduction.

For example, men tend to be more focused on physical attractiveness in potential mates because it could signal good genes for their offspring. Women, on the other hand, often value qualities like status and resources in a partner because it could mean better support for their children.

These differences don't apply to everyone, of course, but they're patterns that have emerged from our evolutionary history.

C. The Influence of Culture and Society

Cultural Variation in Mating Norms

While our evolutionary history sets the stage, culture and society add their own twists to the mating dance. Different cultures have their own rules and norms about dating, marriage, and relationships.

For example, some cultures might encourage arranged marriages, where families play a big role in finding a partner. Others might embrace love marriages, where individuals choose their partners based on personal feelings.

These cultural variations show how flexible our mating strategies can be. We adapt to the norms and values of our society while still carrying those deep-seated evolutionary instincts.

The Impact of Technology on Dating and Relationships

Now, let's fast forward to the digital age. Technology has transformed the way we find and connect with potential partners. Online dating apps, social media, and video calls have made it easier to meet people from all over the world.

But this technology has also brought new challenges, like the rise of online dating scams and the pressure to present ourselves perfectly on social media. It's changing the way we navigate the complex world of mating, adding new twists to the age-old dance.

In this chapter, we've explored the intricate dance of mating, from the biological basis of attraction to the influence of culture and society on our relationships. It's a fascinating journey that reveals the deep connections between our evolutionary past and our modern romantic lives. So, whether you're searching for love or simply curious about the science behind attraction, remember that the dance of mating is a story that's been unfolding for millions of years, and you're a part of it!

Chapter V: The Dark Side of Survival and Mating

In this chapter, we'll delve into the not-so-pretty aspects of our survival and mating instincts. It's a fascinating, and sometimes challenging, journey through the dark corners of human behavior. We'll keep things straightforward and engaging, so everyone can explore this intriguing terrain.

A. Evolutionary Explanations for Aggression

The Evolutionary Roots of Conflict

Picture a time long ago when resources were scarce, and survival was a daily battle. In these harsh conditions, conflicts were a common occurrence. But why did our ancestors sometimes resort to aggression?

Aggression, the act of being physically or verbally hostile, has its roots in our evolutionary past. When resources like food or shelter were limited, competition could get fierce. Those who could defend their territory or claim the best resources had a better chance of survival and passing on their genes.

So, aggression isn't just random anger; it's a survival strategy that has been hardwired into our brains over millions of years. Today, we may not be fighting over caves or hunting grounds, but our instincts for competition and conflict still influence our behavior.

Mate Guarding and Jealousy

Now, let's explore the world of jealousy. Have you ever felt that twinge of jealousy when someone flirts with your partner? It's a common emotion, and it too has deep evolutionary roots.

Imagine you're a cavewoman or caveman, and you've invested time and energy into a relationship. Jealousy could be a way to protect that investment. It might have kept our ancestors vigilant, ensuring that their partners didn't wander off to mate with someone else.

In modern times, jealousy can still rear its head when we feel a threat to our relationships. It's like an ancient alarm system, reminding us to guard our bonds with loved ones. While jealousy can sometimes lead to unhealthy behaviors, it's a reminder that our emotions have ancient origins.

B. Deception and Manipulation in Mating

The Evolution of Deceptive Strategies

Now, let's shine a light on deception. Throughout our evolutionary history, individuals have sometimes used deceptive strategies to gain an advantage in mating.

Imagine a male bird that displays colorful feathers to attract a mate. Those feathers are like a form of deception – they make the male appear healthier and more attractive than he might actually be. This strategy increases his chances of finding a mate.

Humans have their own versions of deceptive strategies, from telling white lies to dressing up and exaggerating their qualities to attract partners. It's not always about being dishonest; sometimes, it's just about presenting the best version of ourselves to improve our chances of finding a mate.

The Modern Landscape of Deception in Dating

In the modern dating world, technology and social media have opened up new avenues for deception. People can edit their photos, use filters, and craft idealized online personas. It's like the digital version of those colorful feathers.

While these tactics can help individuals stand out in a crowded online dating scene, they also raise questions about authenticity and trust. It's a reminder that our ancient instincts for deception still play a role in the modern mating game.

In this chapter, we've explored the darker side of our survival and mating instincts. From aggression as a strategy for resource competition to jealousy as a way to protect relationships, and from the evolutionary roots of deception to its modern manifestations in dating, these behaviors remind us that our past still influences our present. It's a complex tapestry of human behavior, where the light and dark sides are both part of our evolutionary heritage.

Chapter VI: The Future of Survival and Mating

Welcome to the exciting frontier where the past meets the future! In this chapter, we'll explore how technology and artificial intelligence are reshaping the landscape of survival and mating. We'll tackle complex questions and ethical dilemmas without getting too tangled in jargon, so everyone can join in on the conversation.

A. The Influence of Technology and Artificial Intelligence

Online Dating and AI Matchmaking

Imagine a world where finding the perfect partner is as easy as a few clicks on your phone. Well, welcome to the world of online dating and AI matchmaking. Technology has revolutionized the way we meet potential partners.

Online dating platforms use algorithms and data to suggest potential matches based on your preferences and behavior. It's like having a personal matchmaker who can sift through thousands of profiles to find someone who might be a great fit for you.

But while technology can broaden our dating horizons, it also raises questions about authenticity and connection. How well can algorithms truly understand the complexity of human relationships? Can they capture the spark of real-life chemistry?

Genetic Engineering and Reproductive Technologies

Now, fast forward to a time when science allows us to tinker with our genetic makeup and control our reproductive destiny. Genetic engineering and reproductive technologies are pushing the boundaries of what's possible.

Imagine a couple who can choose the traits they want in their future child, like intelligence, athleticism, or even appearance. It's like designing a custom-made baby. While this may sound like science fiction, it's a topic that's gaining traction in the real world.

These technologies offer incredible possibilities, like preventing genetic diseases or enhancing human potential. But they also come with ethical concerns about playing with the building blocks of life. How much control should we have over our own genetics, and what are the potential consequences?

B. Ethics and Moral Dilemmas

Consent and Genetic Engineering

Imagine a future where parents can make decisions about their child's genetic makeup before they are even born. It's a powerful idea, but it also raises important questions about consent.

Should we have the right to make these decisions for our children before they can speak for themselves? What if the child grows up and wishes they had been given a say in their genetic destiny?

The ethics of genetic engineering involve navigating these complex questions and considering the rights and autonomy of future generations.

The Balance Between Freedom and Determinism

As technology advances, we walk a fine line between freedom and determinism. On one hand, we have the freedom to shape our lives, our relationships, and even our genes. On the other hand, there's the risk of losing some of the randomness and unpredictability that make life rich and surprising.

Imagine a world where AI algorithms predict who you should date, what job you should have, and even what you should eat for breakfast. While this might streamline our lives, it could also limit our ability to make choices freely.

Finding the right balance between using technology to enhance our lives and preserving the essence of what makes us human is a challenge we'll face in the future of survival and mating.

In this chapter, we've explored the exciting and sometimes challenging frontier of technology's influence on survival and mating. From online dating to genetic engineering, and from consent in genetic decision-making to the balance between freedom and determinism, these are topics that will shape our future in profound ways. It's a journey into uncharted territory, where the decisions we make today will impact the world we pass on to future generations.

Chapter VII: Embracing Our Primal Instincts

As we reach the end of our journey through the fascinating world of evolutionary psychology, let's take a moment to reflect on the key insights and enduring lessons we've uncovered. This conclusion chapter will tie everything together in a way that's easy to understand and relatable to everyone.

A. Revisiting the Evolutionary Perspective

We began this journey by embracing the evolutionary perspective on human behavior. This perspective is like putting on a special pair of glasses that allows us to see how our past has shaped who we are today. It's a lens through which we can explore the deep-seated instincts and behaviors that connect us to our ancestors.

Throughout this book, we've learned that our survival instincts, such as fear and the quest for resources, have ancient roots that still influence us in the modern world. We've explored the intricate dance of mating, from the biology of attraction to the strategies we use to find love and build relationships. We've also delved into the darker side of our instincts, like aggression and deception, and discovered their evolutionary origins.

B. The Enduring Relevance of Survival and Mating

One of the key takeaways from our journey is that these survival and mating instincts are not relics of the past; they are living, breathing forces in our lives today. While we may no longer face the same life-or-death challenges as our ancestors, the principles that guided their actions continue to shape our thoughts, emotions, and behaviors.

Our brains are like a library filled with millions of years of survival and mating stories. When we feel fear or attraction, when we compete or cooperate, when we form bonds or experience jealousy – these are the echoes of our evolutionary past reverberating in our present.

C. Embracing Our Primal Instincts in the Modern World

As we conclude our exploration, it's important to recognize that our primal instincts are not something to be feared or suppressed. Instead, they are part of what makes us human. These instincts have allowed us to adapt and thrive in a wide range of environments and challenges.

In the modern world, we have the opportunity to embrace our primal instincts consciously. We can acknowledge our fear and anxiety, recognizing them as signals to pay attention to our well-being. We can appreciate the beauty of attraction and love, understanding that these feelings are deeply rooted in our biology. We can navigate the complexities of aggression and deception with awareness and empathy, striving to build healthier relationships and societies.

In essence, understanding our evolutionary past empowers us to make more informed choices about our future. It allows us to recognize that while we are products of our history, we are also architects of our destiny. We can choose to honor our primal instincts by using them as tools for growth, connection, and personal development.

So, as we close this chapter and our journey through the world of evolutionary psychology, remember that you are a remarkable product of millions of years of evolution. Your instincts are not limitations; they are invitations to explore, understand, and celebrate the incredible complexity of being human. By embracing our primal instincts in the modern world, we can continue to evolve and thrive in ways that honor our past and shape a brighter future.

About Freudian Trips

Welcome to Freudian Trips, your dedicated platform for diving deep into the world of psychology. We are more than just a YouTube channel or a book publisher. We are a beacon of enlightenment, making complex psychological concepts accessible and engaging for all.

Our YouTube channel is a rich repository of psychology made simple. We take the profound and often complex ideas from the world of psychology and break them down into digestible, easy-to-understand content. From the foundational theories of Freud to the cognitive insights of Piaget, we cover a broad spectrum of psychological schools and thoughts, making psychology accessible to everyone, regardless of their background or prior knowledge.

As a book publisher, we take the same approach, transforming intricate psychological theories into comprehensible narratives. Our books are not just collections of words, but vessels of wisdom that make psychology approachable and relatable. We believe that psychology should not be confined to academic circles, but should be available to all who seek to understand the human mind and behavior.

At Freudian Trips, we believe in the power of curiosity and the pursuit of knowledge. We are here to stoke the fires of your curiosity, to guide you on your intellectual journey, and to help you navigate the fascinating world of psychology.

If you are someone who is not afraid to question, to explore, and to learn, then you are in the right place. Join us on this journey of exploration, as we make psychology easy to understand, one concept at a time.

Be sure to visit our Youtube channel at: www.freudiantrips.com/youtube

You can also visit us on the web at www.freudiantrips.com

Welcome to The Freudian Trip community. Stay curious. Stay enlightened.